MOTHER MINOTAUR

poems by

Sarah Ahrens

Finishing Line Press
Georgetown, Kentucky

MOTHER MINOTAUR

Copyright © 2026 by Sarah Ahrens
ISBN 979-8-89990-359-5 First Edition
All rights reserved under International and Pan-American Copyright Conventions. No part of this book may be reproduced in any manner whatsoever without written permission from the publisher, except in the case of brief quotations embodied in critical articles and reviews.

Publisher: Leah Huete de Maines
Editor: Christen Kincaid
Cover Art: Matthew Benrus
Author Photo: Nikita Artinian
Cover Design: Elizabeth Maines McCleavy

Order online: www.finishinglinepress.com
also available on amazon.com

Author inquiries and mail orders:
Finishing Line Press
PO Box 1626
Georgetown, Kentucky 40324
USA

Contents

Part I
- Mother Minotaur ... 1
- Incus, Malleus, and Stapes ... 3
- Chorus ... 5

Part II
- Labyrinthos ... 9
- The Lift ... 10
- Origin Story ... 12
- Even Odds ... 13
- Boundary Wall ... 15
- What They Don't Tell You ... 16
- Metamorphosis ... 17

Part III
- Hide & Seek ... 21
- Circle Time ... 23
- Vertigo ... 25
- updates@academia-mail.com ... 27
- Icarus's Mother ... 28
- Dreamer ... 30
- Observer ... 31
- Learning to Read ... 32
- When Ariadne Visits ... 34
- Asterion ... 35
- Punch Line ... 36
- updates@academia-mail.com ... 37
- McGuffey's Eclectic Spelling Book, Revised Edition (1896) ... 38

Part IV
- The Labyrinth's Heart ... 43

Part V
- Retrace Your Steps ... 47
- Ariadne's Bedtime Story ... 48
- Sleepwalking ... 51
- Sing Me Now Asleep ... 53
- Lock Down ... 54

updates@academia-mail.com 55
Basement Storage.. 56
The Radiator... 57
In My Dream 60

Part VI
Theseus Enters the Labyrinth... 63
Wall Follower 64
Agon 65
The Boat... 67
Wave 68
Invocation.. 69
The Red Thread.. 70

For Robert

Part I

Mother Minotaur (after Man Ray, 1933)

You would think after all these years
I would know how to get out.

Of course I wandered,
heard the birds singing outside

and thought: anything is possible.
But that wasn't my story.

It's mostly dark here when I walk
the labyrinth's winding passageways,

except when I see them,
those who come for me

inside my house body.
They say they are an offering,

a tribute from across the Aegean.
They say I have a naked bull face

with proud nipple eyes fixed
forward in the middle of breasts,

tired from being on alert.
I say take me with you, take me

back to the beginning so I can rest.
At least, that's what I think I say

from my mouth abyss,
the space above the scars

where my children were taken out.
When they don't understand,

my bleached arm horns spread
into elbow hooks, ready to lock.

I swallow them so we might
escape together one day.

I was going to be someone else,
someone who framed photographs

and hung them on my house,
in my body. But I can't leave

now that there are
so many people to hold.

Incus, Malleus, and Stapes

Barely visible behind
the stretched, pearlescent

eardrum, lie three bones:
the incus, malleus, and stapes.

We hear the song because
they draw in the drumming,

the beat of bedtime stories,
tides rising and falling.

Named for their shapes,
they are: the anvil,

the hammer and the stirrup.
This is how I hear you

when the ultrasound wand
presses its magic across

my round, tight belly
and its waves crash into yours.

It knows your location.
You're there, there, there.

The movement of your heart
inside me rushes your blood

among reeds by the shore
of your growing, steady and new.

The waves beat
the drum beats
the hammer beats
the anvil beats
the stirrup,
bringing

your sound back
into my body,

spiraling down
in cochlea whorl,

a labyrinth
filled with water.

Chorus

Hey Google, what's the scientific name for the wolf spider?

The district evaluation team did not conduct a thorough assessment, nor provide documentation of how they determined eligibility.

Lycosidae. Some people ask: do wolf spiders spin webs? Would you like to know the answer?

He has difficulty regulating his emotions especially during challenging tasks.

Do you want mac and cheese?

Also, Mom, do you know the lattice method?

Please turn the volume down.

What's the lattice method?

He picks up a purple dry erase marker and starts to draw on the whiteboard.

Will we all get COVID again?

I pour dark, slick coffee beans into the grinder.

Do you have a fever? How many days will you have to stay home? Has the inhaler expired?

I have also included the Zoom link and a copy of your procedural safeguards.

Also, Mom, everything is powered by the sun, even those coffee beans.

While the removal of services may have been appropriate, this is not clear.

The three branches of government are like rock, paper, scissors.

I'm working, honey.

A butterfly begins as a cat on a pillar.

I'm going to try to do this with my eyes closed.

Also, Mom, the happy, the sad: they turned into flowers.

This discrepancy could contribute to frustration and anxiety.

Fire ants could find themselves under attack.

Do you know what a SMART goal is?

Try four square breathing.

A dog's whiskers can detect an object's size, speed, and shape through vibrations.

Specific, Measurable, Achievable, Relevant, and Time-Bound.

Thank you so much for your patience.

Try putting it in a hot air balloon and watch it get smaller as it floats away.

Why does everyone always talk about butterflies when they talk about metamorphosis?

Other creatures go through it too.

Part II

Labyrinthos

What's the difference
between a maze and a labyrinth?

I can't remember,
so I keep looking it up.

A maze has many possible paths,
not all leading to the center.

They say that some
are dead ends.

A labyrinth has only one path
that leads to the center.

They say you can't
get lost in a labyrinth.

But long ago these words
meant the same thing:

a labyrinth was a maze.
There's one inside your ear

with canals and chambers,
and a vestibule with a window

next to a spiral shell
curving in on itself

like an ammonite
fossil in a Cretan cave.

The Lift

You are thirteen years old and the smallest on the synchronized swimming team. They asked you to join because you somehow already knew how to do one of the fundamental figures: the ballet leg. You diligently learned more: the flamingo, the swordfish, the barracuda.

Draw in your breath like making a wish before you blow out your birthday candles, enough for another year. Stretch out on the water's surface, then hinge at the hips and close like an oyster shell sinking to the bottom of the ocean. Rise slightly, until your pointed toes are just below the surface. In one swift motion, thrust your legs straight out of the water and push up to become perfectly vertical. Once the waterline reaches your thighs, glide down with control under the water to finish.

You practice three times a week and start to have trouble with ear infections again. They were so bad when you were younger that you had tubes put in twice (maybe three times, your mother tells you). On the operating table, they put a mask on your face and you started counting backwards from 100. Your dream was a flourish of playing cards and when you woke up you had cotton balls in your ears.

After every swim practice and before you shower, you put drops in your ears to kill any lingering bacteria. The older girls take showers with their swimsuit tops down. Unbound, their breasts are so many different shapes and sizes. One tall, skinny girl, the one whose solo routine is best, always stays in the shower longer than anyone else. You look down at your new breasts, safely tucked away in your Speedo, and wonder when you will have the courage to pull your suit down.

At one point during the team routine, all eight girls are deep underwater. One is parallel to the bottom of the pool, facing down. Six girls swim below her and position themselves: two under her ankles, two under her hips, and two under her shoulders. The smallest girl stands on top of her back, and steadies herself by placing her right foot at twelve o'clock and her left foot at nine o'clock. The six girls whirl their legs around like an eggbeater and push the flattened swimmer's body up, raising the standing girl out of the water.

The lift almost never works. You stand on her back, emerge from the water, and try to strike a pose your coach choreographed to the Dr Who soundtrack. But when her hips are too high, or her shoulders too low, you fall.

You get more ear infections. You go to a special doctor who puts something like a whipped cream can nozzle in your ear and fills it with foam that hardens. They use this mold to make you ear plugs. You understand they are expensive, but they don't fit very well and you can't hear the underwater speaker with them in.

During practice, one of the ear plugs falls out and sinks, as if pulled by an invisible thread. You quickly swim down as fast as you can to try and catch it, glimpsing your blurry reflection in the observation window about halfway down the diving well. The ear plug keeps falling and you feel the pressure of the water asking you whether it's worth it.

You have to let it go. You put your arms above your head, pull them down to your hips as hard as you can, and kick to the surface.

Origin Story

Yours was my third pregnancy,
though I was childless.

As you swam in me, I swam
in bright blue pools every week.

My favorite stroke: forward crawl
for four, then backstroke for four.

Something inside started
to pull inner earward,

and my eardrum sank
into a concave bowl

collecting dust
and skin cells,

wreckage left
behind by the waves.

Even Odds

When I started bleeding
from my ear, the doctor said

everything's fine.
Don't worry about it.

But I did.
I'm good at worrying.

Another doctor took one look
in my ear and said I needed

to see someone else.
Five months later,

a third doctor said
your eardrum is infected,

you will need surgery,
and there's a 50% chance

the infection has spread
into to your skull.

I imagined him
sailing into my ear,

loading his vessel
with seasick cells,

and sailing out
to another port.

So, those seemed
like good odds.

Do you consent
to have student doctors present?

Yes.
Is there a chance

you could be pregnant?
Yes.

The doctor moved the surgery
to the summer solstice.

I didn't know
he would save my life.

I didn't know
he would lose his a year later.

Boundary Wall

She slid the thin blue curtain
across a metal-grooved ceiling

and I answered all her questions
using the words I'd learned:

retraction pocket, canal wall,
mastoidectomy, tympanoplasty.

She looked at me over her reading glasses
and said, are you a nurse?

I'm scared of the anesthesia.
Is there a chance of dying?

Honey, you've got to have one foot
in the grave to worry about anesthesia.

Someone rolled my bed through a maze
of doors and double doors.

White lights became darker and greener
where students in scrubs slouched

against a boundary wall.
Move over. Lift up here.

And my body reacted dutifully.
A voice said, think of a happy place.

Where is it?
Where is your happy place?

I didn't want to answer.
I was almost there.

Before going under,
I said, "Springtime."

What They Don't Tell You

You will wake up before they take the tube out of your throat.

You will vomit in a silver bowl after riding the elevator.

You will always put a vaseline-covered cotton ball in your ear before taking a shower.

You will never put your head underwater again.

You were lucky the infection didn't breach your brain.

Metamorphosis

Temporal bone
hewn, no longer

standing guard
in front

of the brain.
Ear canal

widened
into a cave.

The hammer
lost.

The anvil
lost.

I cannot
determine

location
from sound.

Stalactites drip
in the distance.

Where am I
in this place?

Where does this
passageway go?

My hoof-hand
smooths back

wild hair,
horns lower,

and my tail
marks time.

Part III

Hide & Seek

I hear a humming
coming from
something
that sounds
like the boiler,
which I know is
on my right
but I look left.

My children call for me

    A particle hides part of itself.

and I go into a room

    It knows where it is and how fast it's moving.

and they are not there.

    But we can't know both things at the same time.

When I concentrate, I realize

    The more we know about one,

that the sound's source is still unidentified,

    the less we know

unknown, not connected to any thing.

    about the other.

Where are you?

Extractor fan, husband
loading the dishwasher,
talking, music on.

      No chance of finding

a missing sound
with my distant ear,
pocket of loss, an ocean
surging, but never coming in.

Circle Time

All the mothers sat
criss-cross applesauce

on primary-colored carpet.
All the children sat

still on chairs made
of their mothers' legs.

My hands were on my knees,
slightly cupped and facing up,

holding space for you.
Twinkle, twinkle, little star,

how I wonder what you are.
Everyone in the circle sang

and copied the group leader,
our fingers undulating beams of light.

I kept looking at you
over in the corner, watching

and not watching, away
in your own songland.

Up above the world so high.
You know this song,

we sing it almost every night.
Come join the circle

like the other children.
Like a diamond in the sky.

I didn't understand, didn't know
that it would be five more years

of mistaking your distance

> hiding behind me, gripping the back of my shirt when meeting new people, not making eye contact, crouching under a desk at the school open house we insisted you attend

for defiance.

The song ended and I closed
my eyes, not wanting to look

at the other mothers
looking at my empty lap.

Twinkle, twinkle, little star.
I am made of what you are.

Vertigo

When the old door
inside my ear

decayed,
they tore it down

and made a new one
of finest fascia.

Dead skin cells
still gather

on the doorstep
waiting for wax

to move them
toward the light,

but it never comes.
The instrument

that draws them out
cools and convinces

my inner ear
to tell my brain

that I'm falling
out of an airplane

without a parachute.
I dig my thumbnail

into my middle finger
as a distraction.

As I spin,
I try to remember

what it was like
underwater,

feeling lighter,
moving slower,

becoming a current,
my long hair soft

seaweed, swimming
as many lengths

as I could without
coming up for air,

escaping the burden
of gravity for a while.

updates@academia-mail.com

Is this publication yours?

Help us keep
your profile
up to date.

Did you write
"First, Do No Harm:
Impact of the Transition
to Integrated Curriculum
on Medical Knowledge
Acquisition
of the Transitional
Cohort"?

The author's name
is the same as mine.

Did I write this?

Icarus's Mother

You've probably never heard of me.
Some women lose their names,

and some give them up.
You probably know my son.

He's the one who dreams
and doesn't listen to his father.

Before he fell, he fell
in love, the first flush kind.

She rushed into the workshop
like wind catching in an unfurled sail

and swiftly wound her way
between statues whose shoulders

turned to widen her path.
Daedalus didn't look up

from his drawing
and Icarus puffed his chest

like a bellbird about to sing.
I know what you've been told,

that my husband gave Ariadne
a clew, a ball of string,

and she gave it to Theseus,
so he could find his way

out of the labyrinth.
But think about it.

When Daedalus was imprisoned
in the labyrinth he himself designed,

he couldn't remember how to get out.
The only thing he knew to do

with thread was bind feathers
into wax wings unfit for flying.

I took her to my loom
and showed her how to follow

the path inside the pattern.
Empty space will speak

the way if you listen.
We are always and never lost.

Some mothers lose their children,
and some give them up.

Dreamer

Eighteen months old squealing
with delight every time I sent

a matchbox car hurtling down
the honey-glazed hallway.

30-piece puzzles every afternoon,
then lining up all the blocks just so.

Two years old seeing the space
where an object wants to be.

My new bed goes over there, mama.
Four years old tying shoelaces

doesn't make sense.
Five years old can't put things

in a rucksack fast enough
at the end of the school day.

Six years old having trouble
paying attention in class.

Seven years old looks lonely
during recess. *I watch the movie*

of my dream in my mind.
Eight years old crossing

the street with eyes closed,
talking about the Permian

period in paragraphs.
The teacher complains,

your kid is a dreamer.
I tell her we need dreamers.

Observer

Waves wave we know
we can't know.

The waves know this.
We watch the waves

and our watching changes
where they wave.

Someone is speaking.
Reverberations float

for a moment and then
disappear. I think

if the sound repeats
I can try to find it.

Learning to Read

The day the magnetic board
came home in a large plastic bag

with a glider at the top to keep
the small letters of the alphabet

from getting lost, you wondered
why they weren't all there.

Meted out once a week
like communion wafers,

they promised it would all
make sense at some point.

The way letters sound, learn that,
put the shapes and sounds together

and move on to the next.
I sent notes back to the teacher

in the reading journal:
these look the same

    b   d
    p   q

upset is quest.
No response.

Instead of Dick and Jane,
early reading books

featured Biff,
Chip, and Kipper.

Fish and chips.
Bish, bash, bosh.

Memorization was a strategy
to guard against

making a mistake
ake ake ake
not
not
wanting to—

you threw the book
against the wall in tears.

When someone finally
listened, she said

the problem is noise,
not sound.

When Ariadne Visits

When Ariadne visits
we play hide and seek.

She finds me every time,
and then I hide again.

When she leaves, the sound
of wanting to go with her,

of wanting to be her,
weeps out of me.

Next time, Asterion,
she says.

Asterion

Metamorphosis is a myth.
Nothing changes

the soft fibers
between your spine

and shoulder blade.
I have to resist

the urge to confess:
there are messages

in those webs
we wipe away.

Punch Line

You say, why is that joke funny?
I say, because the punch line

is surprising, unexpected.
You close your little fingers

into a fist, thrust your arm out,
then extend your pointer finger

and draw a line on the table:
punch line.

I begin to build you a boat
to sail across the water,

to carry meaning
from one word to another.

Gone overboard, you say.
Seal the deal, I say.

updates@academia-mail.com

Did you write
"Priorities and Outcomes
for Youth-Adult Transitions
in Hospital Care:
Perspectives of Inpatient
Clinical Leaders
at US Children's Hospitals"?

McGuffey's Eclectic Spelling Book, Revised Edition (1896)

On the inside cover,
my great-grandfather wrote,

If my name you wish to see,
look on page 103.

The word miss signifies to err,
to go wrong: misguided, mistake.

I stole the smooth, pink stone
from Gina, who lived across the street,

youngest of ten children.
One of her sisters was supposed

to watch us but never did.
We listened to "I Am the Walrus,"

and she said, "Paul is dead."
The man-beasts on the album

cover petrified me.
The pebble-sized stone fit

perfectly in the palm of my hand,
a cotton candy clouded jewel.

I wanted it, I wanted to sleep
with it beside my bed.

With the treasure in my pocket,
I made my escape step by step

down the worn carpeted stairs.
At the bottom, it slipped through

my pocket's hole and pinballed
down between corduroy and leg.

Shame picked it up,
stole it a second time.

I'll give you an apple,
I'll give you a date,

if you will look on page 48.
De signifies down or from:

detect, decipher.
I check for chalk marks

on light posts, letters
in a hidden safe, handkerchiefs

dropped, skeleton keys
left behind, hotel register signatures.

On the sidewalk near the mailbox
I found a piece of pink paper

torn in half, fuzzy yellow
duckling in the corner,

and a handwritten note:
"To use when my fingers r gone."

If you want to go to heaven
look on page 97.

Con signifies with or together:
connect, conjure.

When we dig down
to the root, we find

a maze has many mothers,
many etymons with embryos.

Hard to see them all clearly
except "amasian," which looks

like *maison* and mansion,
a house full of echoes.

Part IV

The Labyrinth's Heart

frustration stomach aches avoidance eating lunch alone for months trying to blend in starting over sensory spirals visiting places ahead of time lock laces checking in again and again thoughts getting stuck school meetings advocates therapists podcasts books Google searches acronyms referrals neuropsych evaluations data standard deviations twice exceptional we've never seen scores this high on the test brush teeth put on deodorant hugging not hugging showing up visual schedules reminders making cookies for teachers explaining training action plans the Principal losing it emotional toolboxes stopping their fist from hitting their head pandemic anxiety covering bases just in case snow days meltdowns come pick him up from school early the more you practice the easier it will be he needs a day off cradling the space just outside of your head something out of reach if you knew a little more got another opinion you would be a better mother your kid isn't sleeping how can you write when they're hurting you don't see you don't see you

Part V

Retrace Your Steps

Go out the way you came in.
It's what all the stories say to do.

Breadcrumbs, red thread, whatever
it is, just work your way back.

My mother reads magazines backwards.
My son wants his bedtime stories read

aloud in reverse, word by word.
But it doesn't work in the labyrinth.

Every step looks the same.
I stop and lose time.

Lichen grows where my fingers
made grooves on the walls.

I write notes to myself,
but can't read them.

I tear notebook pages out
leaving ink trails veering off

the jagged edges
of an arcane map.

Ariadne's Bedtime Story

The first time I met Daedalus,
he dangled puppets

in front of my eyes
while my father fitted

a harness to his back.
We all have them,

and his shined gold.
The puppets danced as if alive,

and I danced with them.
He said I was so good

he would make me a floor
where each stone swirls

a body into motion.
Do you remember

when I taught you
how to dance?

Slide, then stomp
and pivot.

He told my father
he was no murderer,

just misunderstood.
My father felt the same

about himself, called
Daedalus a brother,

and asked him to hide
you, his secret, my sister:

conjure a labyrinth
to put her in her place

and keep her from the light.
As he built, night after night

and all the nights together
seeped into these walls

like black ink darkening
a skein of yarn.

But I found my way in,
I found my way to you,

followed the hoof map
of your heart print.

The stories say, I fell
in love with Theseus.

They would say that,
wouldn't they?

Don't worry,
I love you too.

Don't worry
if you see

something red,
frayed and throbbing,

something beautiful
is coming.

Something beautiful
is going to happen.

Don't worry,
I love you too.

Sleepwalking

There's a noise
at the end of the tunnel,

and for a moment
I wonder if it's coming

from inside me.
Then I hear it again—

small, syncopated footsteps.
Sometimes he comes

all the way to the edge
of my bed before I hear him.

Other times he walks down
a flight of stairs, stops

in the kitchen, and stares.
The sleeping child

and the dreaming child
have switched places.

Try not to wake them.
The dreaming child

doesn't remember
getting out of bed

or how he got here.
I guide him upstairs

and he glides, as if drawn
by a magnetic force, a beacon

fire blazing on the shore.
When head touches pillow,

the dreaming child sinks
and the sleeping child surfaces.

Sing Me Now Asleep

Where is my mother
in the labyrinth?

I get out of my canopy bed
and walk barefoot down

the damp hallway.
She's in her room asleep,

and when I try to wake her
she is Ophelia handing out

rosemary and columbines.
She has other families, quarrels

with Oberon, learns to dance
in pointe shoes, and burns

at the stake sometimes
twice in one night.

She read tarot cards
each morning before

I was born and ruled
Egypt for a whole year.

She's still dreaming,
so I draw the blanket

up to her chin,
its wool fibers

bright red
against her skin.

Lock Down

"Can I have some cranberry juice?" the seven year old asks as I type this.

He doesn't have questions about the virus. He wants to hug me, kiss me, sleep in my bed. The teeth next to his front teeth are missing, making his mouth seem wider. He talks and sings and repeats comedy routines I let him watch that contain swear words.

I stand, pull up my underwear and jeans together, and turn to flush the toilet. When I look down on the back yard, a thin beam of morning light cuts across the window's wire screen.

It flares and says follow me.

I say, breakfast is ready dry tears lose weight pour the tea hold everything.

It's all echoes and no maps.

I can't even read a book.

I took a picture of the spines beside my bed, then deleted it.

updates@academia-mail.com

Did you write
"Blood-Based
Genomic Testing
for Newly
Diagnosed Lung
Cancer Patients
to Facilitate Rapid
Treatment Decisions"?

Basement Storage

This is the part of the labyrinth I avoid,
except when Pluto first enters Aquarius

and I'm forced to go down.
I have other things to do.

Spray the stainless steel
kitchen sink with bleach,

wait, then scrub and rinse.
Fix the garbage disposal,

snake the shower drain.
Sometimes houses flood.

The carpet has to come up,
the drywall has to come down,

the concrete has to be cracked.
Move the boxes full of photo albums,

mixtapes, the *Oxford English Dictionary,*
a four-leaf clover, a newborn baby's

death certificate, divorce papers.
Dig the trench, lay the pipe,

cover it up with stones
and the water will run away.

The Radiator

Corner room, Laura Ashley wallpaper,
small purple buds on a white background.

"Think carefully about this choice,"
my mother said.

Our house was over a hundred years old,
and the iron radiator might have been too.

Slate gray, stone cold, sitting silently
under lead-lined windows.

Built up air inside the radiator
needed release, so I learned to bleed it.

Turn the knob until you hear a hiss,
a whistle of warning, then relief.

Rusty water dripped into a plastic bucket
and smelled like dirty pennies

before we cleaned them
in packets of Taco Bell hot sauce.

You're not listening.
I don't have time.

Sometimes I repeat the thing you say
as a question, twirl you around,

and send you away.
I could look forward and backward

in my vanity's three-way mirror,
project myself into a future

different from daybed,
fabric-covered journals,

grave rubbings, calendars
with red dots on days my period started,

one wall covered with every article
I could find about Sandra Day O'Connor.

When it was time, a scalpel sliced
my nine-month belly, marking

the breakthrough place.
Then the wound closed,

sealing other parts inside.
New wood grew, but behind

the place where the skin bark
healed, I'm building up.

What else am I
other than this mother?

I learn a new word this week: swatting.
False alarm for a shooter

at the nearby high school. My children
are taught where to run, and where not to run.

"Ex-Oxford Student Relives Horror at MSU—
Mom, get me out of here."

You're not listening.
I'm not listening?

I'm cold. Time to bleed.
Pull the red threadscar

from your belly and tie it
around the radiator knob.

*Turn and release me
so I can hiss, whisper, sing.*

In My Dream

The outer door broke off
and there was someone

trying to get in.
I pulled the heavy,

inner door and it split
apart like an axe

had just come down
and the planks pulled away.

I tried to put them back together,
but the force made the wood

come off its hinges.
I ran to you.

It was night and I knew
it was you because

you were wearing
your blue headphones.

You were far away,
on your own,

and someone
was coming.

Part VI

Theseus Enters the Labyrinth

When the hand begins to strike
out of time, you cannot

call yourself into being.
We divide the hour

into four parts, and then listen.
There is something about

the exactitude of the event,
whether we witness it or not,

that leaves little room
for the thing to approach slowly—

for recognition to actually come.
Premonitions are dismissed

because the instruments
would have to be reset.

Wall Follower

I imagine myself as a bird,
morning still air, but

I don't know enough
about instinct building.

I can't leave the fledglings,
and murmuration is a mystery.

Which way did I take
walking back from your house

at 4am after taping a note
to the door, *green green youth?*

Which parts part,
which ones do I have

to leave behind?
I keep turning left.

Agon

I smell Theseus before I see him,
rusted iron laced with chlorine.

The stories say he's come to end
the sacrifices by sacrificing me.

You know the type: pretty boy,
had a paper route as a kid,

makes speeches at dinner parties,
sleeps in a single bed.

He found me, or did I wait
for him all this time?

I didn't know he would look so tired.
He walks toward me holding

a red thread that runs
through the labyrinth,

stretches into the spiral shell,
past the eardrum to the diving well,

all the way back to the beginning.
Or is this the beginning?

He sits down, cross-legged,
and closes his eyes.

I sit across from him and watch.
I think maybe this is enough.

I think maybe I will scream,
but my children would tumble out.

I have to keep them safe inside.
When he opens his eyes,

they look like inlaid mirrors,
his eyelids blind wood.

I see myself inside myself,
staring out from each dark pupil.

And in that moment, which is
the same as this moment,

I know I am the house,
the mother, the bull,

the keeper, the kept.
Theseus blinks

and hands me the thread.
He gets up slowly, one body

part at a time,
like a marionette,

and walks away.
When I open

my mouth to speak,
my children climb out

and follow the thread
out of the labyrinth.

The Boat

It is night, sunset the color
of blue headphones.

Take the boat I made
from the dream doors

that split apart and broke.
Take it to the other side,

drop the axe, and pull
away the planks.

Hinge what you
need inside.

Wave

Hold, hold, hold
the space.

    They turn
Listen and breathe.

    They are turning
Hold yourself like still water.

    They are turning into
Reflect the summer moon and wait.

Theirs is not your story.
So you sit with the beginning,
    their beginning

of not knowing
them until they
know themselves.

Wave and watch them walk.

This not knowing
is loving is
trusting is
holding

the space they made
inside of you
by coming out.

Invocation

My Grandmother
was May Queen

when she married
a sun god.

She gave up drawing
what she saw

through the microscope
to raise daughters

who could make
different choices.

I thumb her talismans
like a worry stone,

and wear her dress
to my wedding.

Its ivory fibers
are woven into

the red thread still
pulsing in my hand.

I hold it close
to my ear,

like a seashell,
and listen.

It starts to speak,
and I start to write.

The Red Thread

I am umbilical,
ancient with afterbirths,

a warp and weft
of artery cords

and vessel fibers
echoing your early

heartbeat, braided
with breath.

I want to tell you
what I saw.

I want to tell you
what I heard.

Acknowledgments

A handwritten version of "The Red Thread" appeared in *Poetose* and was nominated for The Pushcart Prize.

Thank you Christen Kincaid and Finishing Line Press.

Thank you Dr. Saumil Merchant (1960-2012), Dr. Emily Stucken, Sylvia van Meerten, Samantha Shanteau, Stephanie McKeith-Shaker, Amber Karkau, Alexis Boyden, Emma Briggs, Kelly VanEe, Chelsea Knight, Morgan Ragazzone, and Megan Warfle for your profound care and transformative support.

Thank you Sarah Mesle for all the texts, phone calls, Zooms, and ardent enthusiasm about this project.

Thank you Sabrina Orah Mark for your magical midwifery that helped birth this book.

Thank you fellow writers in SOM's Obsession Workshop, especially Jess Richardson for invaluable insights on an early draft.

Thank you Betzy and Mike for your friendship and design expertise.

Thank you Matt for creating such a gorgeous cover.

Thank you Richard and Priscilla for your love and encouragement.

Thank you Robert for that snowy walk home on your birthday and for always believing in me: "Your shoulder blade, your spine / Were shorelines in the moonlight."

And thank you to my kids for being your beautiful selves. You amaze me every day and it is the honor of my life to be your Mom.

SARAH AHRENS began writing poetry in Mrs. Mueller's eighth grade English class at Shortridge Junior High School in Indianapolis, Indiana. She holds degrees in English from Emory University (BA) and Cornell University (MA, PhD). She has taught literature and writing at Cornell University, Auburn Maximum Security Prison, the University of Pennsylvania, and Harvard University. A Pushcart nominee, her poetry, creative nonfiction, and academic essays have appeared in *Poetose, Longridge Review, Modern Loss, The Washington Post, Avidly* (a *Los Angeles Review of Books* channel) and *Romantic Circles*. This is her first poetry collection.

www.sarahahrens.com

www.ingramcontent.com/pod-product-compliance
Lightning Source LLC
Chambersburg PA
CBHW030056170426
43197CB00010B/1547